To Lose & to Pretend

poems

Chris O. Cook

Brooklyn Arts Press · New York

To Lose & to Pretend: Poems

Copyright © 2008 Chris O. Cook

All Rights Reserved.

No part of this publication may be reproduced by any means existing or to be developed in the future without written consent by the publisher.

Acknowledgements:
I wish to thank my 5th grade teacher Julie Schneider, my high-school English teachers Honey Kern, Maureen Ackerman, and Jack Umstatter, my undergraduate and graduate writing instructors James Kimbrell, P.F. Kluge, Marvin Bell, Dean Young, James Galvin, and Robert Hass; my best friends Geronimo Chelius, James Downing, Tom Young, John Wheeler-Rappe, Ben Keene, Brian Puckett, and Scott Kenemore; Samantha Kipling, Megan Anderegg-Malone, Laura Lee, and Helena Fitzgerald; and my invaluable editor, Joe Millar—*ill melee, or fab bro*?

"Will Run Like Rabbits for Food" was first published in *Free Radicals: American Poets Before Their First Books* (Subpress, 2004).

"Big Long Now" lyrics (Cobain/Novoselic) from *Incesticide* by Nirvana; shared © The End of Music, Primary Wave Tunes, Grohl, Novoselic. *Fun for All, the Children Call* takes its quote from the article "Sea Monsters" © Virginia Morell, *National Geographic*, December 2005.

Published in The United States of America
by
Brooklyn Arts Press, LLC
154 N 9th St, Suite 1
Brooklyn, NY 11211
WWW.BROOKLYNARTSPRESS.COM
INFO@BROOKLYNARTSPRESS.COM

Library of Congress Control Number
2008926873

Cook, Chris O. / To Lose & to Pretend: Poems
ISBN-10: 0-9788257-2-1
ISBN-13: 978-0-9788257-2-0

SECOND PRINTING

Cover design by Underground Political Backlash Arts.

for my father,
Gerard J. Cook

Contents

God as a Thing, or Whatever It Is..9
Velvetine Intestine..10
Admirable Fooling...11
Relatively Small Destroyer..12
The Trees Are Just Fine...13
I Summoned Am to Tourney..14
Beginning with a Line from Mitch Hedberg...15
Loud and Bored..16
For Oh! I Don't Know How Long...19
One! One Poem! Ah, Ah, Ah!..20
Weneht..21
Hallowe'en 2004...22
Paris & Helen...24
Simony Says...26
Pretending You've Got a Sliver..28
Decades...29
Driving around on the Roof..30
Lots of People Are Round..31
Pull the String...33
Freeze All the Candy..35
A Dream with a Cliff in It..36
Omigod It Was So Funny We Were Like Cracking Up...37

Good Loser, Nice Life	38
Light Comes on Slowly	39
A Blond Hair on a Black Shirt	41
It Has to Be Keeks So It Will Rhyme with Cheeks	42
A Real Yo-Yo	43
White Gets Underfoot	44
Will Run Like Rabbits for Food	46
Last Thanksgiving before Turning Twenty-Four	47
The World with the Ghost Lake	48
Mancy	50
Last Thanksgiving before Turning Twenty-Seven	51
About the Flower	52
How My Memory Got in My Pajamas	53
Fun for All, the Children Call	55
Non, Je Ne Joue Pas au Tennis	57
I Was Like, Don't Waste Your Match	58
I Just Need a Few Things	59
Drum & Bass for Weird Andy	60
Dancing with a Mailman	62
5.1.189	64
Ending with a Line from the *Victoria's Secret* Catalogue	65

God as a Thing, or Whatever It Is

Ever since I stopped believing in God
I've been pretending I was in a movie.
Early in the morning doesn't feel like it in July,
with the empty beer cans storying the porch
& spent bottlerockets dry-humping the gutters.

Jobs are retarded. The hipster merch-girl at the midnight show
in black jeans & white heels argued that *corsetiere* refers
to the corset-wearer, not the maker. Maybe it's the only thing
where the wearing is harder. Well, that & Poetry—
which means you're a Poet too if you got this far.

You may already be feeling your organs start to shift.
Even though I can prove God has no gender
I'll still fantasize about teachers for the rest of my life.
You run out of underwear fast when you help people move.
You find out what Poetry isn't: You run through

the high-school diary, the college lecture, the grad-school puzzle—
then for a few years it feels like rain every Sunday.
There's no article of men's clothing that makes women horny by itself.
Poetry makes women horny but God doesn't. Suck it, God.
When you move somewhere, you go to bars alone.

Velveteen Intestine

The flirtatiously smug empath with the bob near the papasan
took her time in late Summer comparing my soul to the age
when she'd wrap, to the light of one unshaded lamp, herself
in garbage sacks, pretending they were leather.

Parties are like involuntary debates over belief in talent.
It's time I started dealing with the fact I won't be famous.
When you see me, apologize. I'll apologize back.
Faith is the easiest thing in the world

not to have, so cut it out already. Get to the point
where the language eclipses the grating like rising dough;
where the Poem is a grey cat that acts like it wants to be petted
but doesn't. Gangster-flip an oversized coin skewed *guilt* & *shame*.

Skim it down your culture like a dimmed Hall of Fishes.
Wait for it to once-around & back up your spine.
Girls imagine wearing things & boys imagine touching them,
only most things aren't being touched most of the time.

When Edna Millay was 24 she cut herself with a stage
knife somehow over the heart in Synge's *Deirdre of the Sorrows*,
then later became like a story someone tells about how
there used to be a rosebush in some certain place.

Admirable Fooling

There are more Good Nerds in the world than Evil Nerds,
& that's why Evil will one morning lie buried
like broken toy guns beneath snow & sawdust.
I can get away with the word *heartbreaking*
because I used to cut myself making paper wizard hats
with a whoop-jug, before passing through the hedgerows
to seek out the other gifted children.

The first was Rufus, deadliest on the seaboard with a crayon
but only if you cooperated. He had a real record player.
The last was also Rufus. He retired undefeated
to a mysterious island. Every Sunday
he sends a few jokes I never get. If the world were my dream
people would worship waterslides & chill with rhinos.

You wanna die? Simple. Put on a Star
Wars movie & do a shot every time something comes
across as a double entendre. I want to know
how old you have to be to start calling people "son,"
because the world isn't anyone's dream.
Whenever it's a month, I'm amazed it's that month
& it's, like, always a month.

Oh World, are you onto something or on something?
Oh World, if you've got questions, we've got dancers!
World, the thing about a whoop-jug is,
we're bound to brim it with what we love.
Oh & World...when I save you, there'll be this one part
where I jump a bridge in a speedboat. It's gonna be so cool.

Relatively Small Destroyer

Before anything else, I'm going to need you
to calm down. That was breakfast in the Candle District,
sun across a grating, three girls with runner calves
calling Thomas Jefferson a hottie. The trick
is to compete at not playing.
          Either
there's something to everything, or most things are nothing,
so spare me your "real" problems. The trick is to lose
so much you never lose. I'm not denying friction—
the '90s kids are finding cares, but then still dye our hair
& lie down in the kitchen. You're too good for this

& you're too good for that. I love you with all my heart.
This past Summer people drove white cars around like sex
didn't sell. I bet you noticed. I bet you save champagne foil
until there's nowt to make from it but knives.

The Trees Are Just Fine

The pizza guy turned out to be semi-retarded
& asked if we could talk about the Bible
when he arrived in the rain. It was perfect.

Once every September, at dusk, on Hole #7
of the Oak Brook disc-golf course, the sun sits blinding
at the head of the gauntlet of pine trees perfectly

while dishwater blondes perch like Vargas girls
in the needle-duff, taking pictures of large mushrooms
& laughing in accents that are perfectly hard to place.

(When someone says "It was just too perfect"
about something funny, the funny thing is that
if it was funny, that means it wasn't perfect.)

God is either perfect or looking for an excuse to kill.
It was raining on pizza day, but it wasn't raining
on a lot of other days when nothing happened,

& once, you happened—having been up 'til then
your own gauntlet, Bible, camera.
When you love someone like I love you,
listening to the rain counts as conversation.

I Summoned Am to Tourney

It's not that I don't "get" your untouched canvas—
I get it, but it sucks. While mean, jack in the bungle,

we're up all hours drawing girls sewn up in ivy;
can't stop wishing they'd roller the room red.

You know who "they" are—in that dream where I'm Napoleon,
they make me fill out a report, in triplicate. Hell,

I've heard the soldiers' horror stories about having to shoot
the third bear to enter the bar, because he was strapped with a punchline,

& sure, I gave your cork-wedged girlfriend dexedrine
to make out with another chick, but check this thing:

If you're a formalist, my presence was immaterial;
If you're angry you're po-mo & must leave this villa.

Kepler was impressed that Brahe had his own castle.
Brahe was impressed that Kepler could play "Twenty Flight Rock."

The "blue van" was a myth, but that dream where I'm Hamlet
except the audience has it memorized & yells over me

was real—a real dream. It's now officially a moral obligation to hate
people with talent. If I'd had the slightest idea that *Girls*

Gone Wild was a thing you could invent, I'd have invented it—
but, you know, *nice*. Is this every struggle ever?

Mike says that guy's always got his dick out, you know?
The coolest one is the next one who leaves.

Beginning with a Line from Mitch Hedberg

But isn't *every* picture of you a picture
of you *when you were younger*? At Smith & 9th
I thought the shredded newspaper was a dead pigeon
until the wind took it. Murder, Words, & Well
are all spoken 3 times in a row in *Hamlet*,
a little charm for the inexorable.

                                         I didn't know
that deadly nightshade grew in Brooklyn, up trellises—
the flowers laid out like the universe dying a heat-death,
even curved a little like time. Susan bought me
a root beer & brought me to Prospect Park. That morning,
from Danny's place in Greenpoint, I'd walked out to buy a towel
& realized there aren't many places you can buy a towel.
All in all, Fall felt like there was no such thing
as temperature.

No-one really ever asked for any of it.
No two people believe they're in the same story.

A student first asked me the opening question
of this poem. It made me laugh all day.
Almost nothing had made me laugh since I'd gotten back
from New York, the *Free Radicals* reading at St. Mark's Church
with its flat graves. The editrix was tall & pale.
A lot of tall, pale girls write Poetry. I like
trains, *Hamlet*, trees, baths, Fall, tall pale girls, & saying *editrix*.
That's about everything. My other student is a dancer,
but everyone expects comedy because he's a boy.

Loud and Bored

I.

Were Long Island some guy his purposeful head
  would bend him. His crook'd & unallied
legs would serve him a dry limp. Non-ironically,
Walt Whitman Mall is where his heart would be.

It's Fall as much as any other season—
  the Cross Island Parkway, its joggers & green signs
unfamous enough for a Beginning Credits; a maze
    that puns on the future passive form of praise.

Maybe I got so lost I overlapped
  the Top 40 gender wars; their *Omigod boys/girls suck....*
It was bacaneggancheesawpepakechup
 while drifting between a breakdown & a nap:
It was eight years of edits, with all the reasons
only mine in the light of advance reports of you.

What we'll never know's whether I was ever in the Museum
    while you were in the Museum too, with everyone's puffy coats
                  being held by everyone's Mother—
    every kiss in the Museum deserves another.

II.

Malls are discussed earnestly there, their lit-up fountains
   full of pennies, green-striped menthol butts, & faked tears.
At night the trip is as eyes & horizon
  as a book jacket backwards in the window
    of a bus you think you've been on once before. The distances
    of completely hypothetical places like Texas
         resound in their place softly,
      crisp as leafcrumbs in a sweater on a college tour.

Somehow back there it all ends up
   in a diner at three or four. Sometimes
    the lights all around turn red & when

I get it together I can will you there—
just you and me, or you and me & more.

   I can't wait to teach you to play the guitar!

       for how then, from a room with a very old rug,
  high ceilings, & which smells like books behind glass
   the lingering dull approximate "E"
of your placing it down will precede the click of you
     into the kitchen, where I'll leave half my drink:
The long light at last, with all the hot reasons of the Zoo.

III.

One was a butterfly choker & the MoMA's wrath—
 a stretch of Jericho, with its sharp grass
  diving towards Westbury all motels—
    a gnattish halogen knell
when plaid skirts the floor for all that.
      & *awe*, that.

One sixteen, barefeet, twang-twang the nodding
 of an early June—"not there yet" in between
me & the out-of-touch mainstream of the Moon.

Were they all you, already set? Whose worn sandals
  & summersway I dogged
  into that little bookstore? The one in Cape May?
The one that snuck my Byron-cherry? Was it you
  I chased through the forest to
 the sitting-rocks river behind the old seminary?
How much I thought you dressed like you should be!
 jacked up & wisping like soft focus circa 1983.

It was a hale history of porch-perfected clothes.
 A dust-gravity screechlaugh & a knee.
 A finger-painting about how an engine works.
It was ash perched but no Beauty.

My hair was always getting caught in my teeth
 & the clothes I hated never got returned.
  I never could decide on a tattoo
 so men said openly that the angels would sleep if I burned.

IV.

The lock-broke field-shade house was,
    & slowly bursting, summerly so,
   charsticked to a *"we will never die"* expanse.
Next slide please: Cheering children on the tram!
  for the animal who would *not* rather sleep & emerges
    from the hidden home for a little show.

I was handed a poor poem once with flowers
    in the margins blear. That
  was that & then it was all revisited
    in a meadow & all her chatty friends
    begged the European Boy of the Hour
      to say: "It is beautiful here."

I have been called from many truths by girls;
I have been sent to many principles by women.
I've never excelled at sports;
I've never had exactly what you would call
                        clean linen.

You've spurred me you might say one day
    away from all of it—
   the acquired traits; the retrograde motion.
Imagine the land that could support everything.
Imagine the least relevant part of the ocean.

V.

So through this lack entire, it was by a seaside rash
    of bluffing sunlight that just now I thought—
    past the diners mile on mile—
  to have seen you woven just above the dash.

Raise your hand if you fancy a step out of time,
    in the way that pages yellow:
  In the way that waves attack island prisons,
                        just so.

For Oh! I Don't Know How Long

—for Camille Paglia

It's only safer to be feared than loved
if you're the guy in charge. For everyone else
it pretty much sucks, especially if the guy
in charge fears you. A little girl in pigtails
is just a girl, but a grown woman in pigtails
is sexy. And by the way, I'm wearing
blue contact lenses. Well, how were you to know
I was wearing blue contacts if I didn't tell you?

"Don't Worry Baby" by the Beach Boys is
not actually about cars, because the sentiment
preceded cars, although the sound did not.
Jocks, although coordinated, have trouble dancing
because dance seeks to invite capture
rather than evade it. That's why they dance with beers
& always dance up to you from behind—
what's on your ass is what's about your eyes.

The authentic madman doesn't need beer to do
what others need it to. Needing its help neither
for sex nor violence, he can drink alone.
But nobody can drink until he melts.
For this, we all need songs about the water
but always drive there racing whatever we have
against whatever we want—bodies are bins
that help the art to hold the water in,

as are the boys (and that's as Chinese as
this poem will get, despite the *porcelain*
that turns up in most other poems these days,
with *grandmothers*, or *chiaroscuro* things).
We worry, whether skimming over waves
or other people—but art is to *swim*,
& after swimming, gaze before we drown
up at the A-side; at "I Get Around."

One! One Poem! Ah, Ah, Ah!

Once my uncle who stands funny asked me if a million
was a lot. I told him numbers, like sadness or skyscrapers,
are only big or small by what you put next to them.
Approximately one-sixth of the people I invited
to my *Midsummer Night's Dream* Party actually showed up—
but that would have been enough if they were dancing.

Fucking over & again one day becomes Winter,
closer but more oblique the light & heat. In a flowy
magenta skirt a girl is worth six girls. You hear *inordinately*
as an adverb, but hardly *inordinate* as straight-up adjective.
If my heart exploded right now this would be my death poem.
Dickinson made it to one poem less than 1,776.

People think stuff's in the *Iliad* that's actually in the *Odyssey*,
& that stuff's in the Bible that's not in *anything*.
People want there to be beginnings & endings,
& want numbers to mean things all by themselves.
A Master told me Poetry is about beginnings & endings
& that people who like middles should write fiction.

I once tricked a kid named Adam into believing they'd discovered
a new number, & that we were going to have to change math.
I wonder who he thought *they* were.
One day machines will write music.
"I love you" just means "I forgive you for not being perfect,"
& you should never forgive anyone for not being perfect.

Weneht

There's nothing new to say about being alone
until you find a new way of being alone,
in which case, you're not. A cliché is a cross
between a medal & a bug in your mouth.
I've a stitch from booking after fake boy pain.

I knew this guy who was obsessed with Elvis
because Elvis bit off one of his legs in 1976.
He told me, "Some things best take the shapes of jokes
but aren't lies." I told him if a girl has a tattoo
it means she takes it in the butt. He said, Dammit.

Poems are the jokes you don't laugh at until Heaven
would be a good line if there were such a place,
like how there was this one field with a big tower
with a flashing red light, where girls in sweaters liked
to sing & run fast. Sometimes there was a moon.

The Poetess with the watercolor mouth to whom
I sometimes write e-mails full of facts about animals
has a poem called "There Is No Such Thing As Skill."
I forced 100 random people to write poems
with that title, & some were way better than others.

Many of the poems were elegies about turning 30.
I called it new & silly. They said, "In all fairness,
it never meant failure before." I said Dammit.
I pretended to leave the room. People who pretend
to leave the room sometimes yell "I'm done."

Hallowe'en 2004

"And what if excess of love
Bewildered them till they died?"
—W. B. Yeats

The Drama Teacher says *you can't show thinking*.
He only means *it is impossible*.
The class divides—half think it is a *rule*.
The ablest of the Idiots stands & laughs.
He screams: If we *show thought*, what can *he* do?

The principals are anger & direction.
The Idiot King is an arresting director.
The Drama Teacher knows the risk of adding actors.
He must lecture. He mustn't lecture. The anger.
The anger. The stage is overrun.
The Ghost Light is laughed at by everyone.
The Arch holds all its sharpness at its center.
The Arch puts all its weight onto its difference.

He cries *No more lectures* who feels the roots of lectures.
He will bring the class through the Arch, walking beside them.
He cries *No more lectures* who displays the wounds of lectures.
He will chain the class to an Arch several behind them.

The chains are maddening; the options, more so.
He & many, therefore, come to praise the chains.
The chains come to do nothing but be heavy.
The chains aren't even sure just whom they're on.
The chains are *only following orders*.
The Arch casts a shadow longer than the Field beyond.
He never has to not sleep in the Shadow.
He begins to swear the Sun will kill us all.

The complete clock of Arches is the Dome.
The first Domes had an *oculus* at the center.
The strength was all pointed at the empty space.
He points his strength at Words & calls it God.

The Genius invented God to restrain the Powerful.
He wrapped the Sword in Truth & the Sword bent.
The Idiot embraced God to humble the Genius.
He tripped Truth with Truth's footprints by accident.

The is the things that were already there.
He are the many ways of finding them.

He finds that every King is a King's Mask.
He believes something important happens when we laugh.
He feels some things shouldn't count as reasons.
He tries to find ways to show his thinking.

The Moon is enormous & the land is flat.
The fires from town make the sky brighter.
The smoke from town makes the sky darker.
The museums are burning while the class sings love songs.

He lets his heart say something is cataclysmically wrong.
He lets his brain arrange the Stars into an Archer.
The singing is like fighting, which shouldn't be.
He clutches with both hands his pure meat heart.
He groans & is unable to lift his head.
The head is kept by something from falling also.

Paris & Helen

How many stories are the story of one room?
You walked past that open door, it seemed, one time
for every brother your sure thing would run through,
nodding to everyone else at the party & looking
more suspicious at each go, until....

They say whatever she knows, it's more, but maybe
no one's ever counting from the same place.
That's not—that's *never*—to say she isn't Helen;
I mean, *look* at her: None of it seems
to take any effort, except from everyone else.

She's scoffing at something in that issue of
Mediterranean, folded like there's nothing in it to save.
Should you ask? You never ask yourself the right questions,
but maybe this is easier. Maybe she's Helen, or the space
is the space surrounding Helen. Maybe just q,

and if q is true it means some things you've done
in the past could have been a whole lot easier.
Therefore, q can't be true. You'll have the known world
in one room, if you know what I mean. Then there's Time.
What're you gonna stand somewhere, pointing at one room?

Every New Great Hall is a Long Dark Laugh—
it's always coming up through everyone's feet.
Do you want to help, or feel righteous as a blank page?
Historian! Feminist! Shaker-on-horses! You'll never.
Road sign seen in Sparta: PUTTING SIGNS IN POEMS IS GETTING OLD.

She forgets to turn in the timesheet for being Helen
whenever you start to feel like yourself again:
A smartass calling himself *Alexandros*
whenever there's enough people in the one room.
Either seeing yourself as others can't is not a talent

or all of this is bound to work out swimmingly.
So you had one of those moments on the stairs,
leaning & *sort of* trying to break the banister
because you remembered that thing from 4th grade again—
but it doesn't mean we have to cue the music.

What do you claim you can see in the eyes, kid?
Anger? Math? Conflict is cooperation—relax.
How she's sitting is no accident. You can name lots
of accidents, but also lots of things that aren't.
It's tomorrow. Hold the noises & the voices in one room.

Simony Says

I.

I know, to the week nearly, working at the costume store,
when someone I couldn't see passed by with the other Megan's
perfume on (no, the *other* other Megan—*tall* Megan—
though at the time she was the only Megan).

Then, seven years later, John & I leaned back from the bar
& caught the dead bugs in our wet reflections.
He said his beautiful on-again-off-again, who's doing better,
was hassled in a dream to contact the daughter
of a plain-dealing ghost, dead of cervical cancer.
This was no riddle, but included a name, build, & e-mail.
He never says *truelove* about her, & I hardly ever say it,
but who wants a poem where you can't say *truelove*, one word & all?

II.

This summer's shaping up to be great
-ly like the last one—funny web animation & exhaustion;
John playing the fascist in front of strangers, replete with opera;
Scott rubbing his ass on the TV when a judge show comes on.
Ghostwise, I know John isn't crazy, or at least not lying.
This is the guy who leaves whole bottles of potcheen behind my plants,
touched my arm & told me not to worry about the '60s so much.
I've got too few good friends to ditch them for saying impossible things.
That doesn't imply I believe them, but rather
a freedom that scares me, the freedom not to answer.

III.

The composer who betrayed me used to order
"depth charges" & then we'd talk about tests.
You're either out for the answer or a trick.
The streets that summer were unusually thick

& the composer would brag about his wrists
& the questions couldn't be questions we'd seen before
but every question is a question you've seen before.
Sliding boxes within boxes. *Ghosts* are to *e-mail* as...

IV.

When everyone in the whole book went to the movies
I sat on the other side of everyone's coats

& hoped it would be dark when we let out
& it was, but not the right way, which was nice.

I probably ambled away fast from the high yellow lights
in front of someone laughing into a cell phone.

That was the end of me. I drove back slowly,
past a bridge probably, still hearing the music.

Music is a term that gets thrown around a lot
& probably too correctly for me to bother.

Poetry is a bunch of bright paranoid people
frantically making friends with one another.

Pretending You've Got a Sliver

My model of sex was built on chance,
& you always happen to be fucking with me.
Do you want to, like, not be a spaz
for six minutes? There's too much tiny life
to be counted. I woke up not
in college anymore again today, which probably means
that I need you more than any solo car trip needs a song
or miss you like the last allergic misses weeds.

You could say it's about eleven.
If that TV I found could get reception
in this place it would be much, much earlier.
I'm not sure whether there's even anyone here.

All the sad kids want their picture next to a ruin:
Failing that, a secret: Failing that, a weapon.
They're allover some kind of dead crossword
where *across* is bad Philosophy, *down* is bad Chemistry,
& the adults upstairs won't stop talking—
they talked about switching bodies this one night
but that might be the end of love right there.

Some night just now I danced ironically
with a female friend. She let me free
her shoulders in the laxness; trace her hair—
she let me band it to reveal her ears.

It's like our very own tar pits, but with podiums.
This Poem should have taken place outside
from the very beginning. The average anything is gone.
The adult world only exists in the minds of children.
Some people are so angry they never stop smiling.
Me? I've got the big sweater you gave me.

Decades

—after Rimbaud

'50s black, '60s red, '70s green, '80s white, '90s blue: Decades,
more songs than I can name, more deaths than I can imagine.
'50s, a set of tools, cold to the touch, your reflection
drowns in the spaces between the light, your face

becomes many faces. '60s the grilled cheese catches on
fire, screwing bent over a TV between 8-noon on Sunday;
'70s, a basement echo, someone built something before they
died, ran around it in circles, with a thick brace of onion;

'80s, a glowing statue, so concerned it smiles,
hiding among those slow balloons you punch, flies
all over the country telling terrible jokes.

'90s, bluejeans, having forgiven all they could,
receded beneath the skin, taught fairytales to the blood,
we moved like mist around tall stacks of books.

The moon, some times wheaten, face at a baby,
others the clay-dusty crescent of Hannibal at Cannae,
sickly stripes of gasoline link the miscellany,
lock out the forest, hop in bed after hitting the light.

Driving around on the Roof

When I was little I hit & claimed I was a girl.
I quoted lines from old cartoons I didn't understand
to little or no effect. "Put out that light,"
"Don't you believe it," etc. I thought about driving,
but didn't know how when you're in a car
& "Bridge over Troubled Water" comes on, no-one speaks—
then we act like it wasn't because of the song.

I bet there's lots of stuff like that I still don't know.
But don't laugh—I still know more than most people.
Ask me something. Good question. It all started,
like most bad ideas, with a train going by a playground.
Images of beaches & you don't remember where they are,
it'll make you stop walking from time to time,
& all those people you never saw again, they're

either doing okay, or got murdered, or something.
People with my name creep me out—but wouldn't it rule
if there was a hot chick named Chris Cook & I banged her?
People who have something you want just like being mean,
whereas people who are like you want to kill you.
My father's mother helped teach me to like knowing things—
she'd always say, "You see? I learned something new today."

Lots of People Are Round

An imaginary student asked if *Let me catch
you up* was a good opening line. I said, yes,
for a conversation, but this isn't a conversation. Once
& for all: Nothing actually happened to you,
& we already know that people want to talk
to other people, so what else you got?

Me? Technically, I'm the person writing this down,
& it may be no less significant that—before this
was typed—my handwriting looked funny for two reasons.
I could have slept, or written something else,
or you could be sleeping instead of reading this,
you big imaginary teddy bear, you.

My face hurts. Or, it did when I was writing this,
but doesn't because now it's the next day,
or does because I'm old now & it always hurts,
or doesn't because I'm dead. That all depends on
you, & how long it took you to find this.
If you insist, my face hurt because I was cold,

which is also the first reason my handwriting looked funny.
The second was that yesterday I spontaneously spent
five hours on a colored-pencil sketch
of two girls I knew at school, posed like stained glass.
One was fine bright pale, angular, always
wore outrageous heels & was cold, physically I mean,

like I am now, or was. The other laughed so much
you suspected something, had the best-feeling hair, swore
there were angels in every room & didn't like the word *fuck*
so she'd scream, "*Havesexwith* me! Oh, God, *havesexwith* me!"
I didn't sleep with the first one.
Maybe I could have, but this isn't about me.

It might as well be about the fact that cigarettes
only make a sound when you're alone.
Maybe you're alone, & your cigarette made a sound
just before you read that. Even if you don't smoke,
you're almost certainly alone, because who reads in groups?
Or, if you think it's some kind of rule or something

that a poem by me—which this didn't have to be—
have things in it about me, I could just as easily mention
the time I was walking around at 2 AM
& trying to find a bar because I had to piss,
& when I ran towards a storefront full of neon beer signs
it turned out only to be a store that sold neon beer signs,

which was closed. That's as much like something from a movie
as a beautiful girl who drinks too much & hardly eats,
if you think it's a rule that things be like things from movies.
If you're wondering which girl that was, it was both of them.
The thing about things in movies is, they have to either be visible
or someone has to tell you. This is all a thing I'm telling you,

but that doesn't make me a protagonist,
because nothing actually happened to me either.
That means I'm not naked & I'm not crying.
I'm not starving & I'm not covered in filth.
It isn't three-thirty in the morning on Christmas Day.
My mother isn't in a world of pain because of me.

Pull the String

"When an oake is felling, before it falles, it gives a kind of shreikes or groanes, that may be heard a mile off, as if it were the genius of the oake lamenting. E. Wyld, Esq. hath heard it severall times."
—Aubrey, *Natural History of Wiltshire*

People try to look all these ways in New York.
Maybe we'll all have it together by our thirties,
running up those reassuring grey rocks
in the Park. I don't know what gentlemen prefer,
but geniuses prefer Autumn. Are there better opposites
in English than *deiseil* & *widdershins*?
Everyone should write in form the first few years;
rhymes are a metaphor for something with no sound.

The incense left a column of ash that looked
just like incense. Beware pornography of language
more than of body—it makes you want to write *fast*,
& words done quickly will be the end of everything:
Let Fire & Ice duke it out all they want.
Saints are interesting, but Madonna is a genius—
it's all the same dream, you know, we unhappy few,
& some go one way & some go the other.

Maybe someone will pay me to be the new E. Wyld,
& listen to screaming trees. I nearly lost
myself completely trying to piss those people off
who use Poetry to demonstrate how blameless they are.
That sort of line will never interest me,
but will probably outlive me. Those people
think the best poem is an empty lot. I told them
it was a superstitious, cowardly lot, but no-one got it.

Build something & invite me—I'll describe your eyes
& then stop. It'll drive you crazy. I gave up
describing women extensively in poems;
will say *"forceful wide eyes & fencenets"* only—
the metonymy of fetish has the same roots as Poetry.

I just got up & put a tie on. Seriously.
No mirror—I just faced the wall like it was one.
I think it's the best I've ever tied a tie.

Écrasez l'infâme in 500 words or less,
or use your body while I play a drum.
Probably, everybody would face the wall
if they believed there was a Judge in the wall.
Drums & gavels: Repetition makes it seem
like you know the answer to something. Maybe you do.
Ohh, Baby, your eyes are like the genius of the oak—
but this is far from all you need to know.

Freeze All the Candy

It didn't seem like Summer save for the garbage
exploding with drosophila before snapping shut.
It still ended. Twice in a week I fooled myself
in the bath into thinking there was snow outside.
Mike called & made a joke about my being
at the height of my powers. Laura left

the bra & panties from New Haven, black & white,
bunched up on the green-wire thing in the bathroom
to which I glued dimes to make it even when we moved in.
It made me want her. The Chinese called it *clouds-&-rain*.
The Aztec women-on-the-water dyed
their teeth purple, & only did half their hair.

I wrote two sweet couplets, took a spider outside,
then picked out a t-shirt I didn't know I had.
I found a website devoted exclusively
to pictures of women lying on their stomachs,
propped up on their elbows, knees bent, ankles crossed.
They call it simply "The Pose." The word *romance*

means love now, but it used to mean a story
where magic was involved, & which symbolized Summer.
The difference between sci-fi & fantasy
is that sci-fi involves what's possible eventually.
Autumn & the girls' breasts disappear for 6 months—
the cause, rather than consequence, of hunger.

The young man, as had Issa, climbs the hill.
Pleasure's place is with simplicity precisely
because no-one can ever find it there.
Haiku open or close with the *kigo*, hour & season.
They say it's impossible to write American Haiku.
There was a store in Huntington, New York

in the early '90s. It was called *Copernicus*
& had science things. Some of them glowed,
some of them balanced, others you wrestled with.
You say "I was just getting used to that"
over & over, because it's all you're used to.
It's the only thing you're supposed to be used to.

A Dream with a Cliff in It

When you ask them where something is,
they just tell you what used to be there.

So, I was stuck someplace stuff used to be—
that explains why, once the Spring didn't fix us,

I was about to call Scott & Scott called me.
We watched porn parodies & smoked cigars for a month.

There were all these unexplained dead baby birds
& we both missed Tom.

Tom was either in Nature or in Washington.
The thing about Nature is, shit just kills you.

They hadn't forgotten me. They blocked the street off.
They were grimacing like whitehats & having t-shirts made.

Tom got a vignette through via the old tunnels.
It started in a bar. Scott ran out of sugar.

Coins landed on their rills until Paul McCartney's birthday.
That's when we got the signal to smoke our Masters Degrees.

This just in from the *E!* Channel: *E!*veryone *E!*lse
is still having three-ways on Ibiza.

I'm pretty sure *faint-fainter-nothing* is from something.
If Tom were here we'd filch your rock & paint it.

Omigod It Was So Funny We Were Like Cracking Up

after the egg was ordained a sparkling dropper
but just hung there like someone's symbolic dog.

I guess no-one had to be there.
The kid stares off a bridge at the darkest waves

until they become shark fins. He thinks all danger
should be just that cool. And you know this

one time, at Slant-Rhyme Camp, the Jabberwock
totally denied what he said about Steph,

but then explained it in a way that made it worse.
All August I put off developing

that roll of film, asking about the parking space,
& writing a real letter to Dean.

Everybody I asked about what I'd forgotten
said *The breaks, kid* & wept openly.

Then there was the night I'd never been so uninterested
in so much vomit. That about wraps it up

except for a cellophane lilt, a red-tree echo
of someone screeching *Lick me*, plus some other stuff.

Good Loser, Nice Life

I'm only bothered by picturing the capriciously executed,
not the justly. Wow, that sure was easy to say.
Picturing people is easier than picturing practices
or not, but today at dusk I dreamt about teaching
the guitar to someone—what would be cool is in a basement
with people barbecuing outside. I heard a great joke about
barbecuing in poems—how it gets you into the *New Yorker*.
Funny, so many people would rather barbeque poems.

The weather is the whole world when you're alone
& sometimes people walk around right in the weather.
Karolina brought her Polish nose & long white coat;
I brought my external locus of control.
I've kissed fewer than 100 people.
700,000 people were killed in the Colosseum; you know,
the one the Emperor built to keep them happy.
People walk around, kiss, & die in ridiculous numbers.

I'm sorry for all the years I thought it was just talent.
Just talent doesn't even hold together.
The pun in Shakespeare's heart was "will" & "Will"—
in mine it's "just" & "just." She was more afraid
of the Far Left than the Far Right but still decided at the buzzer
it would be wrong to walk back with me to my hotel
in the buzzing Denver night. Like lackadaisical Summer fingering
on a fretboard, all corrections should be validated by music.

Light Comes on Slowly

Comedy & Love are about remembering things
but so is War. I told her I remembered
what she was wearing, smoking on the porch
in huge sunglasses the first time we met,
but she said she never owned a lime-green dress.
The only difference students will admit
these days between men & women is that boys
recite movie lines more often than girls do.
People call me when they need a movie line
completed or identified, but that's
the only way I'm like a boy. That, &
correcting dresses retroactively.

There are tons of movies all the boys have seen.
There are very few movies all the girls have seen.
Quoting a movie means you think you know
how the room is supposed to feel. Maybe you're right.
Rooms feel cool when they're not yours, only never
as cool as porches, which is why we don't
wear huge sunglasses in them, as well as why
the dresses in them never turn lime green.

The sequels to *Rocky* thought the first one was about
a boxer, when it was actually about a man.
The sequels to *Jaws* thought the first one was about
a shark, when it was actually about a shark.
You never know how cool your own room is.
A man can drink blended eggs for a lot of reasons.
A shark eats a person because it happened to be there.

People call things *tragic* when they're actually *pathetic*
& then yell at anyone who actually remembers things,
but at least they're yelling at a specific person
for a specific reason. Defined by my memories
I was tragic on the porch that afternoon,
& defined by her memories I was pathetic,

but I whispered at her because I knew her room
must be cooler than mine, & probably contained
a single floating dress that changes colors
every time a song from Junior High comes on.

It may be apt but seldom clever to quote
a song, because a song was us the first time,
while movies start apart & weirdly cleave.
We make songs because we're made of movies,
but kids want movies to be made of songs
while the characters smoke—that's the only reason
dresses change color; the only reason your books
look like the books that are *supposed* to be there.

I colored her dress with books. Her sunglasses held
the songs in. She cut her white body to keep
it out of the movies. Her shoes made her legs shake
like the thin beam that shoots by overhead:
First white—then less white—then with drops of red
from behind us to where we were already staring,
smoking a little, bleeding a little,
as if trying to keep from ever hitting the screen,
while the sound comes down the walls like rain on armor.

A Blond Hair on a Black Shirt

Everyone thinks they never do what they always do,
but this doesn't mean no-one is right, or that I'm lying
when I say I saw a hawk alight on an unreachable cross
on an unsettlingly warm November morning
with its back to the English building.

When you don't lie, they call you a liar
all day long, vomgendering a blanket
from the inside out that keeps them
the temperature they didn't know they already were.

Everyone thinks that only they walk a little
faster when they spy a chance
to pluck a spinning leaf out of the air
& that others either don't see the leaf, don't care,
or cheat by running for it at full speed.

It's cheating to be fast.
Most leaves are supposed, the blanket says,
to make it past—more rot, more trees, more chances
to just miss & stare at far-off things in the morning.

What we *want*
is never the leaf but to see
the fastest boy in a heap
reduced to "I tried, I tried, I tried."

It Has to Be Keeks So It Will Rhyme with Cheeks

To celebrate my negative STD tests I thought about buying doughnuts
but then didn't. A week earlier, I'd gotten new frames for
the first time in 14 years, & started wearing my glasses outside.
Then I went back, after a 5-month hiatus,
to writing poems where I tell you about myself.

The fact that you're even reading a poem
means we probably have a lot in common—which is why Poetry
can only accomplish about as much as it does. People still listen
to Dylan because it turns out he was less specific than people
thought he was at the time—or is it more specific?

or that focus is frequently at odds with speed?
I always confuse the specific with the Atalantaesque.
I thought that Laura had said "You're an asshole"
but it turned out she had said "You're an adult."
The problem with the opening couplet

of the Ramones' "Rock 'n' Roll High School"
is that it equates caring about History with wanting to *be* there,
which is not only inaccurate, but represents a larger & more problematic
tendency to regard education as an escape from reality
rather than an enhancement of it—like drugs.

Now might be a Good Time to remind you that
many forms of fun are actually forms of fear.

A Real Yo-Yo

Byron was the first teenager, looming a focus
that blurred the line between suicide & jokes.
I ate dirt 'til I believed in Mastery—
I was alone but it was involuntary.

Ergo my lover's nails; ergo Rock & Roll.
Ergo America with our hands' recoil from the pall.
I've seen you with loud stand swear horrible & refuse
on the ground of limiting your comic cross.

You are all mine as I am all yours,
spiking wet towels over each other's stalls,
my sleeping hand square in your dish of melted ice
while we borrow & send to get personalized

those horrible swears. In love with the indefensible,
we can sit still but everything gets soiled.
If only for the fear of not being killed
we will sell to one another, cry quietly & sell.

White Gets Underfoot

Wait, what? If I'd known we had bubbles,
I could've blown bubbles on chicks' tits & stuff!
There's a cliff with a big wind that comes up it—
people dancing in the Summer leave footprints in grey clay
while the bubbles die onto their sweat, bearing rainbows.
The cliff belongs to the girl I wrote my first sestina

about, in 10th grade, who sat silently & knew the sestina
was about her; who wrote on her backpack, but not in bubble
writing like most girls do, & drew ivy instead of rainbows.
She wrote mostly wavy questions. Her backpack had her pipe & stuff
in it. You might find her in cut corduroys with clay
caught in the cords. She had, like, done it.

I thought I saw her on some stairs in the City
over Christmas, but it wasn't her. The sestina
got made into a t-shirt by some girls—sweated clear on clay
courts maybe; in pools, bogged down, puffed with air bubbles;
lost; ripped for rags; used to wipe up cum—you do a lot of stuff
with a t-shirt, if you have it long enough. Rainbows

are made of people's lost t-shirts. Rainbows
are always turning up in poems but never do shit
for anyone. All of my old stuff
is all over Iowa City. Stuff loops around like a sestina.
It was someone else's before. Couches you have for these bubbles
of time. No more family trees—just couch trees, up from the clay

like the last continue on a hard level. Clay
leaves your life awhile, then these deformed rainbows
of stupid crap you made your parents, bubbled
from burlap—they'll suddenly be sitting
on some shelf; you'll think "God, they're worse than that sestina
was, & those girls even cut stuff

to make it fit on the shirt." You'll want to stuff
all that useless ill-favored red-glazed clay
mess into your dirtiest vein. That first sestina
wasn't very good, but at least it didn't have any rainbows
in it, & I did mean it,
& I guess there were with a word here or there bubbles,

bubbles of where I was headed. Clay becomes something
so pathetic over time. The stuff about the sestina girl's cliff?
I made it up. God, I hate rainbows.

Will Run Like Rabbits for Food

I lied when I said I'd get back to entertaining myself,
  as you can see. There are no teethmarks in the alleyway
or lights on deep through the video store. Only thing
in this town arranged like an opening are my boots—they'd make
              the perfect b&w blownup photograph
at a fiendish thingy, where one lets her hair do the talking.

Whatshername suggested I adopt large lollipops & a new
  posture. I was ballsout about it for eight minutes.
Would you believe I'm shaking?
It's cool—I dreamt I was either dying or concise,
   & not a jot of it was all my fault,
so I hit the couch: Red rocket, red rocket.

The middle bit is booking to church in a galliard,
  reflecting the time I got up, who I started calling, what I needed—
anything tree-tapped would do. I'm talking Hard Science here.
         Okay History—I'll take History—
someday I'll wish I knew more about Rome—
possible't's stuffed up in the days getting longer.

It's an evening that can't even be solved by pointing & laughing
  at books for people who believe in angels. Better to take
a short bath than pack, & a long bath than go anywhere.
It's the new style, that'll see you on the aisle,
  when we're all not ducking ice from our friends in back.
    It's the last bit of tape *vurse* the weight of a saved jeans ad.

Last Thanksgiving before Turning Twenty-Four

Poets should only be allowed to write prose
if they're writing it about another Poet.
Is that a candle, or good bread, do you suppose,
but to one table in this wodelich & inchoate

alignment of apprehension & principle?
Some say the new café deal is in Riga.
Things tend to get a little runcible
on the back porch, where my dress-shoes are invincible

& the dead leaves get dark early. Once,
my good friend couldn't stand it any longer
so he just led us up to every house
we saw. The stories got younger & younger

until, at last, they said fuck it & made
out with the cat. In with the nude. Until
the nude agrees with the stories & drops the charade
down the staircase, along with its last pill.

But it was a splendid smell of newspaper, anyhow—
around the muted game & the iron holders for things
nobody seems to put in holders anymore.
The morning will chill; the daydreams about rings

will bring my appetite back from the less fortunate
subtraction problems, on the brink of a non-importunate
shiny new daydream without a porch in it
where a guy can lean a while, & then sneak it.

The World with the Ghost Lake

"I stepped on their faces because they resembled me,"
wrote, at 36, Anne Sexton of her childhood dolls,
which is funny for an originalboxful of reasons.
Firstly, after three decades of hearing
that it is precisely the opposite evaluation
that compels young girls to obliterate their dolls,
one bends his eyes; one throws his hands in the air.

Hands—when out of the air—can draw things,
in either sense: To *coax* or *represent*,
as water from a well, or as a well on a sign
to let one know a well is near, though not visible.
The drawing is compelled to look like a particular well,
while the word *well* is all wells equally,
past & present, actual & potential.

The man yells about the particular thing he's done,
& the woman about that general class of things.
When you yell into a well it keeps going
'til you find yourself being yelled at by yourself.
You can't draw water—*represent* water—
unless you draw the bucket too, or the movement.
Women define *yelling* by movement, not by volume.

Then there's the little matter of drawing women.
One may only later—or never—consciously articulate
that women's buttons are on the left, men's on the right—
yet may have always drawn them that way anyway.
That, in general, is just how grammar works:
Words words words / well well well.
This is the only time I mention myself in the poem,

myself in particular. A whisper can be a yell,
a scream a whisper. There is no *myself in general*,
unless you consider that Sexton, who was,
actually, in the past, using a typewriter,
left the *y* off the *they*, so on the actual paper,
the last three words are: *The resembled me.*
Here's where light gets yelled at by gravity.

If *resembled* is an adjective, then *me* is the subject—
the center & the actual. If *resembled* is a verb,
then *the* is the subject, & *me* is pure potential.
That's the difference between believing the world
revolves around you & that the world *is* you.
Puns, essentially hermaphroditic, complicate matters,
as in: "People are always leaving the why off the they"—

& accidental puns must be interpreted,
halfway between a drawing & a word.
People use *The Word* to mean both life & death.
Most doll-destroyers have a hard time resolving
the fact that Sexton, who surrendered, was clearly hot.
Though most men would prefer that they draw them
women artists single out & list body parts a lot.

Mancy

The next time the phone rings once & stops meet me
on the saturated hillside overlooking the Interstate,
in flared green cords patched here & again in cheap black lace—
bring a tape player & some old bleached-out cassettes.

There's recidivism en route from this place.
How many times have you stayed up all night?
How many more? Sometimes it makes me angry
when you kiss my neck, other times not.

Somewhere a spider is watching a person watch a game show.
That's always happening in America.
I filled up the black notebook with the Iowa logo

& found a note inside saying someone called about the sadness.
It was someone who got much better, then sad again.
French me. Tell me it's the highway the hill disparages.

Last Thanksgiving before Turning Twenty-Seven

All you get for having no illusions is a medal,
& you don't even get that. I stop at green lights;
I'm bad at keeping in touch with people;
and yes, right now, I am—technically—bleeding,
but don't look so surprised.

There's a reason you don't write poems about not reading
(you can't see them in the dark).
Please, don't apologize—while I was waiting
I learned another way to play C#.

When you don't see Poets for more than a few days
they say, "I thought you were mad at me."
Last weekend I barely recognized Iowa City,

plus everyone's getting married.
The '90s were the first red-haired decade since the '40s.
We need to decide more things in much less space,

like whether irony is a more perfect sincerity
& whether to scream that in everyone's face.
Can we decide in the TV room, if we use trays?

I heard this great line—you know the one,
but we don't think it means the same thing,
which is *fine*. The *problem* is, when I prove you wrong,
everyone calls me an asshole.

It's not my fault; I love cinnamon,
but I don't have anything to put it on.
People like to write songs about how they've been
places. That's cute. It makes people assume
you must've sat still at some point.

About the Flower

Thanks for the flesh-colored flower, if you ever
   gave me one. I do have a memory of it,
    or of something at the corner of a staid desk, right beneath
      the lip-print you put on the switchplate after Christmas.

It's possible I might have found it myself—if it was
   a flower. Possible it was lying in the beaten center
of a soccer field at the height of a useless season,
       & that it had been purple once.

Did you give me no flesh-colored flower & I
   give you no lovely evening? If I had, might you
be there now in the dress you called your *quintessential*
     Megan dress? In the new shoes that filled up with blood?

I'm working on a long poem these days. It was conceived
   after that phone call & so it's the first you haven't
made me promise to dedicate to you. You sat across the table
   in fiction seminar with a lollipop on purpose.

You called me again because you thought I had called you.
I hadn't, but you didn't know anyone else named Chris.
   Does that mean I did call? Or was it the Jack-o-lantern
     that we left when it rotted by the thin river & kissed goodbye?

These days every blessed thing seems a lot like air
   travel. "Everything's an opera," my Dad used to say.
You'd think I'd be as used to it by now as he was,
      or almost as tall, or something.

How My Memory Got in My Pajamas

Would you like to hear what happened after that? After I stared
at the quiver of identical pens hunting some quality
about them to debate? After we ran though the nominal
drugs? After you stabbed me for trying to dress you up
like the aquiline signifieress on the billboard for the old secretarial school?

Nothing happened, but that doesn't mean it doesn't matter.
I bled right through that time of night when every sound
makes you think someone's in trouble. I sat still & thought
hard about eating. I flipped through an article about unemployed elephants.
That's not a nonsense line, but it has to do with Thailand

& it's very complicated. Just forget about it.
I'm sure the elephants will too, because they actually *do* forget things,
just like Poets actually do have to eat, & not just some crazy
metaphysical food like Shelley, or just eggs like novelists.
You'd have looked stellar in the ruffles, & the pencil skirt

would have been too tight for you to conceal the knife.
It takes a train to get me through the Winter.
In Thailand, they still walk under an elephant three times
to ensure an easy birth—but it might just be an excuse
to walk under an elephant, which seems like it would be cool.

In America the elephant is the symbol of the Republican Party,
& if they were unemployed that would be even cooler,
but as Poets already know, being insane is a lifetime appointment.
It's that time of night again, & you still age in the Winter,
even though sitting around feels less like an activity;

less like you're about to do something else. There are no
big words in this poem. I had a list of big words,
but I lost it. If I were people's idea of an elephant
I could find it, & if I were people's idea of a Poet
I wouldn't need it, or food either, & if you were my idea

of the secretary on the billboard, you would do
your nails while on the phone & lose an earring in my sheets.
Nylon was invented in the same moment as napalm
& they were both invented because we were running out of gasoline,
& we're always running out of gasoline, because everyone thinks

they can get through the Winter without help,
except Poets, who run out under the forgetful sky
every time they hear a noise, hungry & bleeding.
Aside from that, we have the same problems you do.
Just look at the monolithic essential orders we all belong to.

I'm packing up my monolithic essential orders 'til the Spring.
The Winter's gay. Especially the creepy spark of December.
I am a clone. Reaching for the dildo before you could say no
was exactly the question of where the elephants should go.
We're in Iraq. I am in Thailand.

Fun for All, the Children Call

*"They thought this mountain was very special. And so
150 years ago, 45 farmers here collected a thousand silver
coins to buy and preserve Lurking Dragon Hill."*
—Cen Zhuxian, guide, Guizhou Province, China

When the voice on the white phone boils over like a bear,
it means Laura's giving me a hug. Then she asked if I wanted
another candle like the one I liked, with the three colors,
but I couldn't remember any candle like that. I could see
the snow in the Walgreens parking lot, & in the narrow garden
of the house between, but nowhere else, not even in the air.

I once wrote that clocks are like razors in the Winter
but I was wrong, because razors mean something. The Right
never liked science, & since Feminism, the Left doesn't like science,
& science is just the sum total of true things.
This means that saying something *means* something is either harder or easier.
That means that this poem is neither "good" nor "bad," but "interesting."

"Interesting" is a technical academic term meaning "not at all interesting."
This poem is not at all interesting, which means it's good,
which is not to say "true," because nothing is allowed to be true.
This goes double for facts, like the fact that Laura's legs give me a boner,
by which I mean that the media give the media a media.
The snow that I can't see may keep falling through this night that doesn't exist,

but the Right & the Left agree about one thing: I shouldn't get boners.
My mom said she believed in evolution, until I told her
that believing in Adam & Eve means you *don't* believe in evolution,
& when I say "I told her" I mean that it took fifteen minutes,
& that she cried the whole time, or would have if my mom could still cry,
but she can't because she hates herself, because she's Catholic,

only she also hates men, but only when she feels
like she's allowed to, which is never, & anyway she just defines "men"
as "everyone besides herself," only she doesn't know she does this,
which, you have to admit, is pretty "interesting," by which I mean "the media."
I want Laura to call back & sing me a song about science.
If I were still allowed to believe in Freud, I could tell you what that means.

They say satire grew out of the awareness of Winter—
the death of meaning; the final at the end of the year.
Oh, by the way, my little horse called—he thinks you're queer.
The fact is, *I'm* Jesus, & I have a boner, & even though
I winterized both the Left & the Right in this poem,
the Left is still better, because we just are.

Non, Je Ne Joue Pas au Tennis

Sticking stuff up your ass makes you a better person.
And stop telling me that adjectives are genocide.
   I think your stupid scarf is genocide, so there.
Yes, I do think I'm a Real Poet.
Yes, I do think I'm smarter than you.

I'd say Let me start over, but I don't want to.
It's coming for me like nine pity kisses.
   Everyone on commercials here is ugly.
   Everyone on the street walks like they feel they shouldn't.
In old horror movies, reporters have guns for some reason.

Remember that time you gave up & pushed a wall?
This is what you were illustrating. If I had a box,
   there would not be room in the box & I don't love you,
but it's not important. What's important ends pretty
early on; that's why it's important. Don't look at me

like you think an Artist can just "rent a movie."
La dee la da da dum. *Oh, drown in a pastry*
   I might have thrown back from a podium. Didn't, though.
How could I have? It never came up.
Now I open all the windows, see that shape in the dust

on my dresser—it's coming & I can't crack my toes.
I've accumulated no pranks, no secret passages or codes.
   I bet it works this way for everyone:
My everyone, at least. My everyone, right at home,
has natural sunlight, orgies, & a hand like ice.

I get a headache when I bite it. It crunches
like the opposite of oyster-snot; gives me that dream
   where there's too much test to carry.
I beg for more, then wink & tear it up sideways.
I beg & tear more test than will fit in the dream.

I Was Like, Don't Waste Your Match

"Spin afraid, instantly grown (?)"
—Nirvana, "Big Long Now"

"Speak in phrase, instead of groan (?)"
—Nirvana, "Big Long Now"

The blown-branch euphoria of sleeplessness,
lying waking into high light, like a stale dorm
with one thrown chair & oral sex for nos-
talgia's sake; snow flat against glass, from

the inside. This snow, conjured by a late
stereo-glow, attendant on it her pink pinkies,
tea & tapestries, hunger. This roommate,
her awful CDs. Heaven & Earth, must I

be a member? Borrow gloves, remember how
to find the echo archway where the chalk hails
he with an untuned acoustic? Allow
I've summat of a flu, be snuck my meals?

It will grow hard with me. An insignificant
provincial adjunct. Truly, I was porn
in a berry bower. Gentles, ubi sunt
qui prope nos biberunt, anyhorn?

If I should sleep now, every good thing
that led from yesterday, without passing go,
may flame of its volition, pose a ring
around me. To it straight: But as for snow,

let it welcome the incense, dying down the door,
or throwing down the die. But let it call
between the music, let me cry, half-sure:
Let me start over—I would make it Fall.

I Just Need a Few Things

Badgers are filling me with lies
is a statement both factual & entertaining enough.
Sometimes I can tell the worth of a poem
going in, by my handwriting, & other times
it's all the solid white sky in a big parking lot,
your hands smelling in December of last December,
still trying to explain things way past lunch.

These septets I'm on this year have me as nervous
as a genius isn't when around a lot of stone.
Look—a slight young woman left her gloves
by the weeded tunnel where the villagers come to blame
me, or slight young women, or me for slight young women.
They call one-by-one, down it, after wars they'd love to name.
I understand you'd like to write a Poem

where it's a boy & girl sitting there the whole time
flirting by comparing whose glasses are stronger,
but the sign by the tunnel clearly forbids that,
right between "campfires" & "skateboarding." Why badgers?
Because as nouns they're fuzzy & surreptitious,
but then turn into verbs & won't leave you alone.
The lost gloves are steadily dampening. You can drink now,

then care so little you make an obvious joke,
which shows you all over again why you love anything.
Here I am, on the way in. We've never eaten
here before, but it smells fantastic, & turns out
we don't know the young woman gloveless in the headlights,
dancing "fake sexy" but cold & careful enough
that everyone exhales like an old-school drawing of the wind.

Drum & Bass for Weird Andy

The unconnected pitch worse than the dead.
It's that way with a jewelcase on the bed
(a CD by my Poetry student's band)
& the Long Island clipping in my hands:
A young man in a skullcap stares & stands
by an unmarked police car, with the trees
that line Lloyd Harbor's stuffy travesties
unclimbable & clucking as they will.
I'll off & on take notice that "The Hill"
's unflaggingly the nickname of each place
I've ever found myself, or tried, by grace
of memory, comparison, or lie
direct. It wasn't, first, an age to try
conclusions, or to let them work their way
along you, though we all had, & would pay
a piece of us out of proportion each
long evening, once long sequent to that beach,
should we chalk up an earlier self more free
from formulas on youth's cold gravity
& playful in his art's nobility.
It fell that way with me when, having cued
the slow track on the demo, a subdued
conceit on partners in despair of meaning,
the matter dropped more pastoral & keening
than a barrage on true love might have gone—
or, second, cold debates on Andy's lawn
amid the ecomilitants who danced
with fists, with visors & enormous pants.

Only what never happens stands forever:
No bricks or other staged attempts to sever
the cooking from the clay expand with all
of potent present needed to unscrawl
the mud beneath the music & the crime;
it boils not skin to, nor apart from time—
our time casts children as, for light or harm,
the *arbiteri elegantiarum*.

One with his music broken down through words;
one noted now as symbol for three herds
of heart, creed, sure—but mainly sore confusion
& irritable reach; some an allusion
to older dignity while most just skate
as blissful as the blood is—as innate
as that bell's bloody whisper, when you wait.
It isn't, third, a crutch now or a chain
the children wear; what's fleckless & remains
is a sententious receptivity
to mercy, rage, & their small ironies.
Sometimes I've not the strength. Always I feel
a sweetness to the wrist behind the deal
regardless of the flop—but it is true
I'd cut & recut once things passed to you.
We choose our battles & our instruments,
if not our ground, or even in which sense
we fight, & which we play. That will appear
once softer sons have knocked a wall down here,
a tree down there, & in the dust betrayed
our errors to us. As for yesterday
it was a time, take it for call & call:
We can't stand or undress it like a doll
but neither can it stare with human eyes
begging a further comment, hypnotized
as if by our own guilt about the sky's
serving as contrast, with its patterned stars,
to what, from some less distance, smells like scars.

Dancing with a Mailman

There's a difference between Beauty & the Train,
on the last obvious hand, but there's also
a difference between Beauty & Beauty, if you follow me,
so follow me. You keep saying the world
doesn't revolve around me, but then can't give me
one good reason why not. I'm getting over Christmas
(It seems like every December I think, Damn,
more famous people must have died this year
than any other; then I forget most of them died)
& into that part of a year when everything cuts you.

It's not a fun cut—not like May, mid-morning,
on a long rural straightaway when you cut
around the mail truck while it's half-down in the thing.
It's clocks—clocks are like razors in the Winter.
I'm always mailing poems, but it's never sexy.
No-one ever gets sexy at the Post Office—
it's like the Doctor's, only you're there constantly
& all the garbage cans are overflowing.
By the end of the poem, I'll have invented a word
involving love & temporality.

Look at it go: A perfect line within a general line:
Like this train (I told you I was on a train already?)
or the memory of twelve legs in a row;
a burlesque show by the Lake, 3 bottles of champagne
with [*some guy who was never really in the poem*].
I was glad at last it was rows & not a bar.
I've nearly had it with bars. I heard a commercial
for one where they bragged that their bands only played
covers. "Damn," people must think, "Original songs?
That's too much like reading, especially in the Winter."

Speaking of translation: At the Zoo,
this one time, a bear was having some difficulty
negotiating his hiding place, & two women behind me
said "Oh, look! He can't get his bum in." The situation
was funny to the women, & the statement funny to me,
but neither one was funny to the bear. I've not nearly
had it with bears—I think they're wonderful.
Matt wrote a great poem about bears;
when he was reading it, instead of *zoos*
he said: "When pandas were introduced to Jews...."

That was funny (it's okay, Matt's Jewish!). So what
have we got so far? Christmas, razor-clocks, a bear;
two women behind me, three bottles, six women in front
equals *36 Ways To Die* in my thrilling new spy novel.
I was like, "He's got a mandolin!"
& everyone at the REM concert knew what was up.
I still haven't involved love & temporality
in a word yet, here on the Train, or here,
the place from which in low light I'm remembering
the Train. Both places. I love it here.

That's the matter with May, you know: It's both places.
That's the matter I gather & the matter I gather you for.
To tell you I've had it with laughing at all of you—
you can go ahead and start understanding things now.
I'm going home. Should I invent Home, here at the end?
The confluence of sexy dancing & Christmas specials?
A dialectic between burlesque & Burl Ives?
Hey, throw it on a letter & see if it gets to me.
I'll be here, in low light, on either no sleep or a lot,
trying to hear the nylon scrape above the ceaseless applause.

5.1.189

Don't play dumb: I know it was you who taught me
to say *tits* to my mom & got me in trouble.
If there were only one book it would be my favorite
possession, but I can barely appreciate
the light hitting them all. Of the light we make film—
film looks one way from Attica, another from Columbine,
though Attica & Columbine are both very pretty words.

Animation styles have changed. Mickey Mouse has looked
so many different ways. You think you knew the same
basic stuff when you were nineteen, but you didn't.
Even before that, the times you were lucky enough
to be in the Woods with girls—you still couldn't
have really written it until remembering
in half & lightly, like the opposite of being sick.

Most people don't acknowledge things about words
or, therefore, themselves—Poets are supposed to believe
Poetry can cure them. I don't know what I believe.
People can take tits, music, Jesus, *anything*,
& club you over the head with it. I guess people like
being clubbed: It makes them feel at home. Home is great,
but Home is also what we need the Woods for.

Ending with a Line from the *Victoria's Secret* Catalogue

I don't want to have to act in front of you.
You could have a hat with both a bird & veil,
but this is hardly a temple. You're hardly a grail,
& neither you nor I is the want of you.
This is nothing to stand on, or beside.
I feel like I got married, & then died.
Those dancing on the table were my guests.
Those pissing in the garden were my priests.
Those carving up your wedge-heels brought the epithets.
Those smoking in the stairwell pinched the bride.
Somewhere is the need for building a sad rest
   with perfect herbs cooked perfectly, or at least
   to amble out i'th' dark & dig the dim roots.
Most of the world is water—The rest is swimsuits.

Chris O. Cook was dragged up on Long Island, New York, starting in 1978. He received a BA in English from Kenyon College and an MFA in Poetry from the Iowa Writers' Workshop. He's worked as a costume-store stock boy, video-store know-it-all, mall-kiosk polltaker, locker-combination changer, standardized-test grader, and monorail conductor. He's taught at the University of Iowa, Kirkwood College, Kendall College, North Park University, DePaul University, and Harper College. His work has appeared in *Free Radicals: American Poets Before Their First Books* and *The Facts on File Companion to the American Novel*. He currently lives in Chicago.

www.ingramcontent.com/pod-product-compliance
Lightning Source LLC
Chambersburg PA
CBHW032050290426
44110CB00012B/1035